REAL
BiOS

LIONEL
MESSI

By Marie Morreale

Children's Press®
An Imprint of Scholastic Inc.

Photos ©: cover: Jean Catuffe/Getty Images; back cover: Lluis Gene/Getty Images; 1: Marc Atkins/Getty Images; 2, 3: Albert Gea/Landov; 4-5: David Ramos/Getty Images; 6-7: Gustau Nacarino/Landov; 7 left inset: Evrim Aydin/Getty Images; 7 right inset: Reuters/Landov; 8: Javier Heinzmann/Getty Images; 9: Escuela General Las Heras/Getty Images; 11: ZUMA Press, Inc./Alamy Images; 12: Horovitz-Pagni/Newscom; 14: Miquel Benitez/Getty Images; 15 top left: Cosmin Manci/Shutterstock, Inc.; 15 top right: Toshifumi Kitamura/Getty Images; 15 bottom: Manu Fernandez/AP Images; 16: Ververidis Vasilis/Shutterstock, Inc.; 17 top left: Molnia/Dreamstime; 17 top right: Miff32/Dreamstime; 17 center: Neil Lockhart/Shutterstock, Inc.; 17 bottom: Juan Moyano/Dreamstime; 18: Scott Bales/Newscom; 21 top: Daniel Luna/AP Images; 21 bottom: Andreu Dalmau/Newscom; 22: Manu Fernandez/AP Images; 23 top: Lluis Gene/Getty Images; 23 bottom: Manu Fernandez/AP Images; 24 top: David Ramos/Getty Images; 24 bottom: AFP/Getty Images; 25: Paul Hanna/Reuters; 27: A.Pauli/Newscom; 28: Ian MacNicol/Getty Images; 30: Metin Pala/Getty Images; 31: Lluis Gene/Getty Images; 33: David Ramos/Getty Images; 34: Juan Mabromata/Getty Images; 35: Europa Press via Getty Images; 36-41 background: conejota/Thinkstock; 36 pushpins and throughout: seregam/Thinkstock; 36 lined paper and throughout: My Life Graphic/Shutterstock, Inc.; 37 blue paper and throughout: Nonnakrit/Shutterstock, Inc.; 37 top left: Zkruger/Dreamstime; 37 top right: Gabriel Robledo/Dreamstime; 37 bottom: Gonzalo Arroyo Moreno/Getty Images; 38: Peter Kim/Dreamstime; 40 left: Chinafotopress/Newscom; 40 right: Allstar Picture Library/Alamy Images; 41: Lluis Gene/Getty Images; 42: Miguel Ruiz/FC Barcelona via Getty Images; 43: Lluis Gene/Getty Images; 45: Karel Navarro/AP Images.

Library of Congress Cataloging-in-Publication Data
Morreale, Marie.
  Lionel Messi / by Marie Morreale.
    pages cm. — (Real bios)
  Includes bibliographical references and index.
  ISBN 978-0-531-22379-6 (library binding) —
ISBN 978-0-531-22563-9 (pbk.)
  1. Messi, Lionel, 1987– —Juvenile literature. 2. Soccer play-
ers—Argentina—Biography—Juvenile literatrue. I. Title.
  GV942.7.M398M67 2016
  796.334092—dc23 [B]   2015025188

All rights reserved. Published in 2016 by Children's Press, an imprint of Scholastic Inc.

Printed in the United States 113
SCHOLASTIC, CHILDREN'S PRESS, and associated logos are trademarks and/or registered trademarks of Scholastic Inc.

5 6 7 8 9 10 R 25 24 23 22 21 20 19 18

Scholastic Inc., 557 Broadway, New York, NY 10012.

Leo celebrates another win with his Barcelona teammates.

MEET LEO!

SOCCER'S SENSATIONAL SUPERSTAR!

Lionel "Leo" Messi first set foot on the soccer **pitch** when he was just five years old. Nicknamed the Flea by his older brother Rodrigo, the little tyke was born to play the world's most popular sport. But way back in 1992, no one had a hint that Leo would eventually become the number one player in the world. They knew he was good . . . but he became much more than that! He is also awesome, astounding, and awe-inspiring . . . and that's just the *A* words!

In this *Real Bio*, you will learn about Leo's early days in his hometown of Rosario, Argentina, and his career-changing move to Barcelona, Spain. You will find out how he became an international superstar, but you will also see his other sides: family man, car enthusiast, food fanatic, and more. You will even find out his mom's secret recipe for his favorite meal, *milanesa a la napolitana*! Once you finish this book, you will be yelling "G-O-A-L!"

Chapter 1

E FLEA JUMPS FROM
ARGENTINA TO SPAIN

LEO WAS SMALL AND YOUNG, BUT HE WAS ALREADY A SUPERSTAR

Soccer—also called football or fútbol—is the most popular sport in the world. There are professional soccer teams on six continents: Europe, Asia, North America, Africa, Australia, and South America. It is especially popular in South America, which boasts many of the game's most legendary players, such as Pelé from Brazil and Diego Maradona from Argentina. The same continent is home to today's best player, Leo Messi, who is also from Argentina.

Even before Leo was born, his father, Jorge, mother, Celia, older brothers Matías and Rodrigo, and maternal grandmother, Celia Cuccittini, were huge soccer fans. And when younger sister Maria was born, she joined the soccer fan club, too!

The Messis lived in the city of Rosario, Argentina. Leo's father worked at a steelmaking company, and

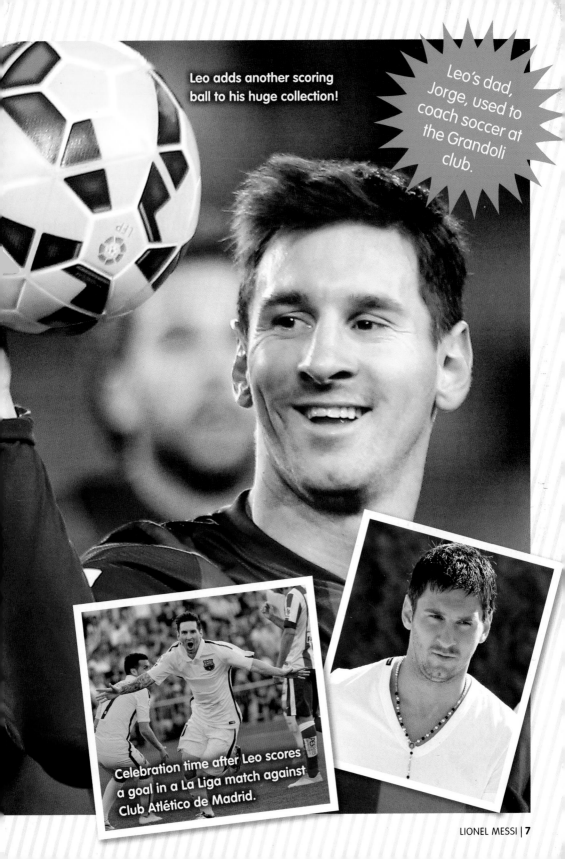

Leo adds another scoring ball to his huge collection!

Leo's dad, Jorge, used to coach soccer at the Grandoli club.

Celebration time after Leo scores a goal in a La Liga match against Club Atlético de Madrid.

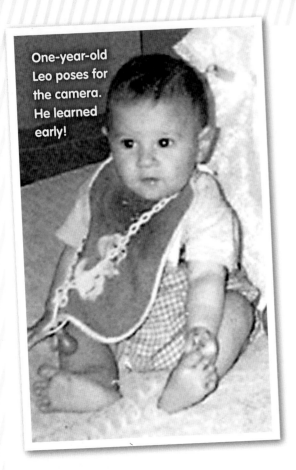
One-year-old Leo poses for the camera. He learned early!

his mother worked at a magnet manufacturing company. They lived in a two-story brick house, which Jorge had built with the help of his father, Eusebio. It had room for their growing family and a backyard so the kids could play outdoors. The Messi house was always full of family, fabulous cooking, and lots of fun. But the one subject that always brought them together was soccer. They loved the game. The kids played it, Jorge coached it, and they all went to watch the local team's matches.

As a child, little Leo was shy. He loved watching his brothers and cousins play soccer, but he spent a lot of his time inside playing marbles. He was small for his age, so his family thought he might have been reluctant to kick a soccer ball around with the bigger boys. Well, that ended when Leo was given a white ball with red diamonds for his fourth birthday. At first, he still didn't join his brothers outside, but he always kept his ball close by. He even slept with it. One day, Matías, Rodrigo, and Jorge were outside playing soccer in the street. Leo hopped in and started making moves. "We were stunned when we saw what he could do," Jorge told Luca Caioli, the author of *Messi: The Inside Story of the Boy Who Became a Legend*. "He had never played before."

Leo must have learned a lot from watching others play soccer, because even at the age of four, people realized he was a whiz kid. "My first memories are from when I was very little, maybe three or four years old, playing in my neighborhood at home," Leo told worldsoccer.com. "I can picture myself with the ball at my feet from a very young age."

Leo's biggest fan was his grandmother, Celia, who took care of him and his siblings while his parents were working. She often took Matías and Rodrigo to soccer practice, and Leo tagged along to watch. When Leo was five, he joined one of the local youth soccer clubs, Grandoli. Leo's grandmother often brought

At five years old, Leo was in elementary school and already playing soccer!

him to the Grandoli pitch to watch the games. On the sidelines, Leo would practice kicking a ball against the stands. Grandoli's coach, Salvador Ricardo Aparicio, noticed his skills. Celia often suggested that Aparicio try Leo on the pitch, but he was reluctant because of the boy's small size. But one day, Aparicio needed one more boy to fill out a team of kids born in 1986.

According to author Luca Caioli, Coach Aparicio asked Celia to let Leo play even though the other boys were bigger and one year older. He said, "I'll stand him over here [by the sidelines], and if they attack him, I'll stop the game and take him off." Grandma Celia claims that she was the one who noticed the team was short one boy and urged the coach to play Leo. Aparicio finally agreed, but in this version of the story, he told Celia, "OK, but I'm putting him near the **touch line** so that when he cries you can take him off yourself."

Whichever story you believe, no one was crying by the end of the game. Especially Aparicio. "[Leo] was born in '87 [but] he played with the '86 team," he told Caioli. "He was the smallest in stature and the youngest, but he really stood out. And they punished him hard, but he was a distinctive player, with supernatural talent. He was born knowing how to play. When we would go to a game, people would pile in to see him. When he got the ball he destroyed it. He was unbelievable, they couldn't stop him."

That's why his brother Rodrigo nicknamed him the Flea. On the soccer field, no one could stop Leo. Well, the little Flea had an itch to make a big name for himself. When he was eight years old, Leo moved from Grandoli to Rosario's famed Club Atlético Newell's Old Boys. His father played there, as did both his brothers. The coaches knew all about Leo, and they asked Rodrigo and Matías to bring him in. Leo started trying out with the club's minor leagues right away. After a month of playing different positions and impressing the coaches, he was placed on a team called the 87th Machine.

Leo (front row, second from right) with his Grandoli teammates and coach.

said to the coaches: 'We have to sign him. Now.' For what did I see? A kid who was very small but totally different from anyone else. He had incredible confidence, agility, speed, great technique; he could run full speed with the ball, dodging anyone in his way without hesitation. It wasn't difficult to spot; these talents everyone now knows were obvious, even though he was just thirteen years old."

Signing Leo to the team wasn't a simple process. There were problems concerning his age and medical condition. Also, he

THE BASICS

Home Sweet Home

Leo still owns his childhood home in Rosario.

FULL NAME:
Lionel Andrés Messi

NICKNAME: Leo,
the Flea (La Pulga in
Spanish), the Atomic Flea

BIRTHPLACE: Rosario,
Argentina

BIRTHDATE: June 24, 1987

PARENTS: Celia and Jorge
Messi

SIBLINGS: Older brothers
Rodrigo and Matías,
younger sister, Maria

WIFE: Antonella Roccuzzo

SON: Thiago

ROLE MODEL:
Portuguese soccer
player Cristiano
Ronaldo

Older brother
Rodrigo shows
off one of
Leo's awards.

BIG BREAK: A video of Leo playing got
Barça interested in him

FUN FACT: Leo can sleep 12 hours a
day!

2015 INCOME: $51,800,000, plus
$22,000,000 from **endorsements**

TWITTER HANDLE: @
Messi_Oficial

FACEBOOK: www.facebook
.com/LeoMessi

Leo was ecstatic when he was named to the 2008 Argentina men's Olympic soccer team.

"WINNING TITLES FOR THE TEAM IS MORE IMPORTANT THAN WINNING INDIVIDUAL AWARDS."

F...
L...

LE...
ANI...

H

any o
interv
next

On h
with t
witho
to wh
accor
happ
You d
happ
stop a

his ne
Argen
move
the FI
Cham
was g
for be
Golde
top sc

Whe
played
senior
exhibi
a year
his lor
debut
main
Liga g

LEO BECOMES BARCELONA'S BEST

THE MAKING OF A LEGEND

FC Barcelona is mostly known for its national team, but the efforts of its junior teams are also highly respected. La Masia (the farm) is Barça's youth academy that prepares the younger players. It is right next to Camp Nou, which is Barça's home field. The junior teams learn the ins and outs of soccer. They practice, play, practice, and play again.

Leo thrived at La Masia. He continued to grow, finally reaching a height of five feet seven inches. He also learned real teamwork. "It helped me a lot because I came [from Argentina] alone, and I was with all the guys in the Masia," he told *Time For Kids*. "We were all from someplace else, and we helped each other. The truth is that there were a lot of happy moments because we were there together for a lot of time, and the relationships between all of us got stronger and stronger. Lots of happy times."

LEO'S SCOREBOARD

FUN 'N' FAST FACTS . . . FAVES 'N' FIRSTS!

THE NAME GAME

BIRTH NAME:
LIONEL ANDRÉS MESSI

NAME CHANGE
ORIGINALLY LEO'S DAD WANTED TO SPELL
"LIONEL" WITH AN E—"LEONEL"—BUT
THOUGHT "LIONEL" LOOKED BETTER

MYTH
LEO WAS NOT NAMED AFTER AMERICAN
SINGER LIONEL RICHIE

MEANING
LIONEL MEANS "LITTLE LION"

FOODIE HEAVEN

MOM'S SPECIAL DINNER
MILANESA A LA NAPOLITANA

DRINK
MATE (A TYPE OF TEA)

SEAFOOD
SCALLOPS

CANDY
DULCE DE LECHE (A SWEET TREAT MADE OF MILK AND SUGAR)

MEAT
STEAK

SANDWICH
CHICKEN SALAD

BAKERY TREATS
ALFAJORES (CARAMEL-FILLED BISCUITS)

FANTASTIC FIRSTS

- Leo is the first soccer player to win four consecutive FIFA Ballon d'Or awards.
- For his first birthday, Leo's aunts and uncles bought him a Newell's Old Boys football shirt.
- Leo got his first brand-new adult size soccer ball for his fourth birthday.
- Grandoli was Leo's first youth team—he was five years old when he joined.
- Leo's first time on the pitch for Argentina's national team lasted only 40 seconds!

CELIA MESSI'S MILANESA A LA NAPOLITANA RECIPE

"I buy the rump or a piece of hindquarter [of beef]. . . . I put a bit of salt on each piece, dip them in egg and coat them with breadcrumbs. I fry them in an oven dish. I slice the onion finely and fry it over. When the onion turns white, I add chopped tomatoes, a little water, salt, oregano and a pinch of sugar. Once the sauce is done, I pour it on top of each piece of beef, making sure they're well covered. I take some cream cheese or hard cheese out of the fridge and lay it on top of the beef in thin slices. I leave them in the oven until the cheese melts. All that's left to do is fry the potatoes as a side dish and the *milanesa a la napolitana* is ready to serve."

"A CHILD'S SMILE IS WORTH MORE THAN ALL THE MONEY IN THE WORLD."

FIRST INTERVIEW

The year 2000 was the last year Leo played with Newell's Old Boys club. Of course, they won the championship. The Argentina newspaper *La Capital* ran an interview with 13-year-old Leo. Part of it included this list:

IDOLS
MY FATHER AND MY GRANDFATHER, CLAUDIO

AIMS
TO MAKE IT INTO THE FIRST TEAM

FAVORITE PLAYERS
MY BROTHER AND MY COUSIN

HAPPIEST MOMENT
WHEN WE BECAME CHAMPIONS OF THE TENTH LEAGUE

FAVORITE TEAM
NEWELL'S

SADDEST MOMENT
WHEN MY GRANDMOTHER PASSED AWAY

HOBBY
LISTENING TO MUSIC

A DREAM
TO PLAY IN THE NEWELL'S FIRST TEAM

FAVORITE BOOK
THE BIBLE

FAVORITE FILM
BABY'S DAY OUT

A MEMORY
WHEN MY GRANDMOTHER FIRST TOOK ME TO PLAY FOOTBALL

FAVORITE TEACHER
PE TEACHER

OBJECTIVES
TO FINISH SECONDARY SCHOOL

HUMILITY
IS SOMETHING A HUMAN BEING SHOULD NEVER LOSE

DREAMS
DO COME TRUE
A LIFETIME OF LOVE!

"Lifting a title makes me feel so happy because it's what I want to do in football: be successful," Leo told *FourFourTwo*. "I find it impossible to single out specific victories, because they all mean so much to me. The Champions League is the best tournament there is, but the enjoyment I feel from winning any trophy is very special. When I was a kid, playing in the streets of Rosario, I'd never have imagined that I'd have reached the level I have and won Ligas, Champions League, and other very important titles. I didn't even imagine that I'd be living in Spain, or playing for a professional club as huge as Barcelona, let alone anything else. That all seemed a long way away for us as a family, but it's exactly what's happened. It's amazing."

What is also amazing is that Leo has achieved so much in his personal life, too. He married his longtime love, Antonella, and they had little Thiago. Always the devoted family man, Leo loves spending time at home with his wife and son, and you better believe he is teaching Thiago some fancy moves. Thiago is already an "official" member of Newell's Old Boys Club. Leo laughed with a reporter from metro951, "I think he's a member of many clubs and he doesn't even know . . . many clubs sent him shirts and member cards."

WHEN THIAGO IS OFFERED A BALL OR SOME OTHER TOY, LEO SAYS HE "ALWAYS CHOOSES THE BALL!"

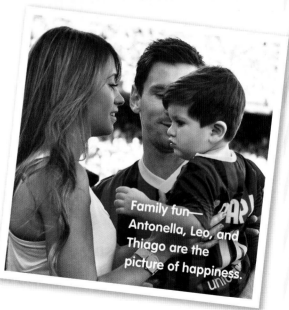

Family fun—Antonella, Leo, and Thiago are the picture of happiness.

Resources

BOOKS

Caioli, Luca. *Messi: The Inside Story of the Boy Who Became a Legend*. Mt. Pleasant, SC: Corinthian Books, 2013.

Jökulsson, Illugi. *Messi*. New York, NY: Abbeville Kids, 2015.

Part, Michael. *The Flea—The Amazing Story of Leo Messi*. Beverly Hills, CA: Sole Books, 2013.

Perez, Mike. *Lionel Messi: The Ultimate Fan Book*. London, England: Carlton Publishing Group, 2013.

Facts for Now

Visit this Scholastic Web site for more information on **Lionel Messi**:
www.factsfornow.scholastic.com
Enter the keywords **Lionel Messi**

Glossary

endorsements *(en-DORS-muhnts)* support or approval of someone or something; famous people are often paid to endorse products

exhibition game *(ek-suh-BISH-uhn GAME)* a friendly athletic competition where there is nothing at stake

hormones *(HOR-mohnz)* chemical substances made by the body that affect the way it grows, develops, and functions

pitch *(PICH)* soccer field

touch line *(TUCH LINE)* a line that marks the boundaries of a soccer pitch

Index

Acknowledgments

Page 9: First soccer game with family: *Messi: The Inside Story of the Boy Who Became a Legend,* 2012

Page 9: First soccer memory: worldsoccer.com May 7, 2015

Page 10: First game for Grandoli: *Messi: The Inside Story of the Boy Who Became a Legend,* 2012

Page 10: Coach Aparicio on Leo: *Messi: The Inside Story of the Boy Who Became a Legend,* 2012

Page 12: Coach Vecchio on Leo: *Messi: The Inside Story of the Boy Who Became a Legend,* 2012

Pages 13–14: Carles Rexach on Leo: *World Soccer Legends: Messi,* 2014

Page 16: Moving to Barcelona: hubpages.com January 10, 2015

Page 18: Winning titles: hubpages.com January 10, 2015

Page 19: Teamwork: *Time For Kids* February 23, 2012

Page 20: Style of play: worldsoccer.com May 7, 2015

Page 22: Diego Maradona on Leo: *China Daily* February 25, 2006

Page 23: Training: *FourFourTwo* April 21, 2015

Page 24: Proud Papa: *FourFourTwo* April 21, 2015

Page 27: Leo on his wife and son: messinews.net

Page 27: Fight to reach your dream: brainyquote.com February 2015

Page 29: On his success: content.time.com January 26, 2012

Page 30: On partying: content.time.com January 26, 2012

Page 30: On being bullied: worldsoccer.com May 7, 2015

Page 31: On preparing for a game: *FourFourTwo* April 21, 2015

Page 32: On how he relaxes: *FourFourTwo* April 21, 2015

Page 32: On young fans: *El País* October 1, 2012

Page 32: On not being a hater: *El País* October 1, 2012

Page 32: On being highest paid player: villyvacker.hubpages.com January 10, 2015

Page 33: On losing: *Time For Kids* February 23, 2012

Page 33: On fans all over the world: *Time For Kids* February 23, 2012

Page 34: On advice from Maradona: *Messi: The Inside Story of the Boy Who Became a Legend,* 2012

Page 34: On being on Argentina World Cup team: *Messi: The Inside Story of the Boy Who Became a Legend,* 2012

Page 35: On Thiago knowing his dad is a star: facebook.com Leo Messi interview with metro951 November 23, 2013

Page 38: Celia Messi's recipe: *Messi: The Inside Story of the Boy Who Became A Legend,* 2012

Page 38: Child's smile: lionelmessibarcelonafc.blogspot.com March 18, 2013

Page 39: First interview: *Messi: The Inside Story of the Boy Who Became a Legend,* 2012

Page 41: Part of a great team: www.brainyquote.com/quotes/quotes/l/lionelmess553568.html

Page 42: Lifting a title: *FourFourTwo* April 15, 2015

Page 43: Thiago and soccer clubs: metro951 November 23, 2013

Page 44: 1 in 11: DailyMail.co.uk June 21, 2015

Page 45: Goals: *FourFourTwo* April 15, 2015

About the Author

Marie Morreale is the author of many official and unofficial celebrity biographies. She attended New York University as an English/creative writing major and began her writing and editorial career in New York City. As the editor of teen/music magazines *Teen Machine* and *Jam!*, she covered TV, film, and music personalities and interviewed superstars such as Michael Jackson, Britney Spears, and Justin Timberlake/*NSYNC. Morreale was also an editor/writer at Little Golden Books.

Today, she is the executive editor, media, of Scholastic Classroom Magazines and writes about pop culture, sports, news, and special events. Morreale lives in New York City and is entertained daily by her two Maine coon cats, Cher and Sullivan.